Sports Illustrated KIDS

FOOTBALL TALK

HAIL MARY, PICK SIX, AND MORE GRIDIRON LINGO

BY MARTIN DRISCOLL

CAPSTONE PRESS
a capstone imprint

Published by Capstone Press, an imprint of Capstone.
1710 Roe Crest Drive
North Mankato, Minnesota 56003
capstonepub.com

Library of Congress Cataloging-in-Publication Data is available on the Library of Congress website.
ISBN: 9781666347104 (hardcover)
ISBN: 9781666347135 (ebook PDF)

Summary: Throw a Hail Mary! Pass the pigskin! Catch a pick six! Discover the meaning of these gridiron terms and more in Football Talk. Created with Sports Illustrated Kids, this nonfiction book presents wacky lingo and puzzling phrases from the football field. Explore the origin of these words and phrases—from touchdown to red zone—and discover how collegiate and pro players use them on the gridiron. With action-packed photos and rapid-fire text, this book is sure to be a solid hit with young football fans!

Editorial Credits:
Editor: Donald Lemke; Designer: Sarah Bennett; Media Researcher: Svetlana Zhurkin; Production Specialist: Katy LaVigne

Image Credits:
Associated Press: Ed Zurga, 25, James D. Smith, 27, Jennifer Stewart, 13, Phelan M. Ebenhack, 19, Tony Ding, 23; Newscom: Cal Sport Media/Charles Baus, 11, Cal Sport Media/Romeo Guzman, 21, Everett Collection, 29; Shutterstock: AlsuSh, 14, ann131313.s, 24, Anton Brand, 6, Chip Harris Design, 8, Dorottya Mathe, 22, DoyanDesign (burst background), cover and throughout, Julien Tromeur, 26, Larry-Rains, 16 (football), Leonid studio, cover (football), cover and throughout (mike), cover and throughout (dotted background), Mechanik, 20, Memo Angeles, 18, Nicoleta Ionescu, 12, parose, 10, Sararoom Design, 28, wowomnom, 16 (ice cream cone); Sports Illustrated: Erick W. Rasco, 7, 15, Robert Beck, 5, 17

All records and statistics in this book are current through the 2021–2022 season.

Table of Contents

TALKING FOOTBALL

A bomb and a buttonhook wouldn't seem to have much in common. They are, however, both names for pass plays in football. A flea-flicker is another pass play. So is a Hail Mary. And the list goes on. Sometimes it seems like pro football has a language of its own. It's a language created over many years.

The history of the National Football League (NFL) stretches back to 1920. The league formed that year with 14 teams. The sport has changed a lot since the Canton Bulldogs and the Dayton Triangles were in the league. Today's NFL includes 32 teams. The modern NFL is the most popular pro sports league in North America.

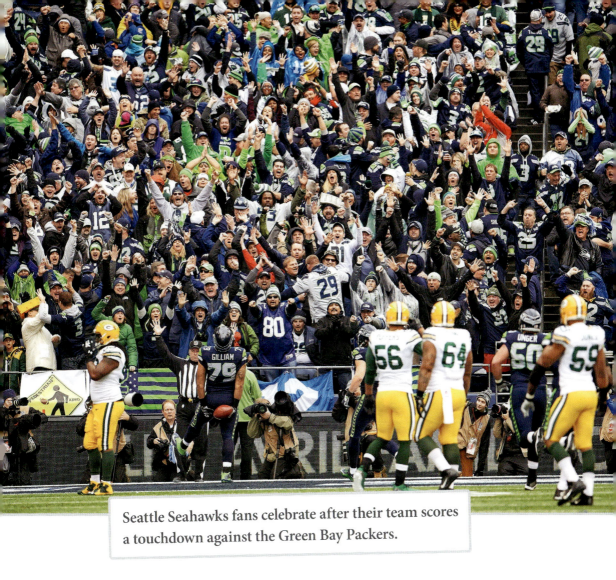

Seattle Seahawks fans celebrate after their team scores a touchdown against the Green Bay Packers.

Millions of fans follow NFL teams closely. These teams usually play only one game each week. That leaves lots of time to talk about every game. And fans do a lot of talking. Same goes for players, coaches, and sports reporters. The words they use can be surprising and exciting—just like the sport they describe. Buttonhooks and bombs are only the beginning.

CHAPTER ONE

TALKING OFFENSE

gunslinger ▶ a quarterback who has an unusually strong throwing arm and who passes a lot

shotgun ▶ a formation in which the quarterback stands several yards behind the center to receive the snap; in a normal formation, the quarterback crouches directly behind the center and gets the ball straight from his hands

bootleg ▶ a play in which the quarterback fakes a handoff but keeps the ball and runs toward either sideline

Green Bay Packers star Aaron Rodgers is a real **gunslinger**. You'll often see him in the **shotgun**. He's also been known to run a **bootleg** now and then. And when he does, he usually gets results. Rodgers is a quarterback, or QB. He's no outlaw. But you might get the wrong idea when you hear talk of his play.

FACT Late in the 2021 season, Rodgers threw his 443rd touchdown for the Packers. That broke Brett Favre's team record of 442. Favre was a top gunslinger of an earlier time in the NFL.

A gunslinger is not merely a quarterback who has a strong arm. A gunslinger is also not just a quarterback who passes a lot. He must be both of those things. He must also be able to fire the ball far down the field and hit a receiver in stride. Rodgers can do that better than nearly anyone.

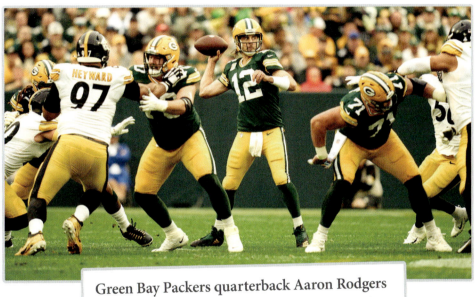

Green Bay Packers quarterback Aaron Rodgers sets up for a pass against the Pittsburgh Steelers.

Rodgers took over as the Packers' starting QB in 2008. Between that season and 2021, he threw 106 touchdown (TD) passes where the ball went at least 20 yards. That was more than any other NFL player. He also threw five TD passes that traveled at least 50 yards in the air. No one else matched that. He once threw a touchdown pass that was airborne for 61 yards.

quarterback ▸ the player on offense who lines up behind the center and receives the ball to begin most plays

halfback ▸ the usual ballcarrier on running plays; halfbacks are often called running backs

fullback ▸ a player on offense who lines up beside or behind the quarterback; fullbacks are usually big, strong players who are effective blockers

Most football fans believe the **quarterback** is the most important player on offense. After all, nearly every play begins with the quarterback receiving the ball from the center. And how well the quarterback plays makes a big difference on game day. It's hard to win if your quarterback plays poorly.

Patrick Mahomes proves how important a quarterback can be. Mahomes plays QB for the Kansas City Chiefs, and he plays the position well. Very well. In his first five NFL seasons, he led his team to the Super Bowl twice. The Chiefs won the big game after the 2019 season. Before that game, the Chiefs had not been to the Super Bowl in 50 years.

But if a quarterback is so important, why does it sound like something less than a **halfback**? And what about the **fullback**?

The position of quarterback got its name long ago. In the early NFL, teams often lined up with four players in the backfield on offense. The quarterback began the play closest to the line of scrimmage. Two halfbacks lined up behind him. And the fullback stood at the rear.

All that has changed in today's game. Often teams line up with only a quarterback and a single running back in the backfield. Sometimes the quarterback has a halfback and a fullback behind him. Only rarely will an offense put four players in the backfield.

FACT What makes Patrick Mahomes special is the way he plays his position. He can stand in the pocket and throw as well as most anyone. He is known for finding creative ways to get the ball to a receiver. He might chuck a sidearm pass. He might toss the ball underhanded or flick it as if passing a basketball. Or he might dive away from a would-be tackler and launch a pass in midair.

wideouts ▶ offensive players who line up farthest from the ball and whose role is to catch passes

hitch ▶ a route in which the receiver sprints straight up the field, then stops suddenly and moves toward the sideline or the center of the field

buttonhook ▶ a short or middle-length route; the receiver sprints straight up the field, then stops suddenly and turns back toward the quarterback

deep post ▶ a route in which a receiver starts running straight up the field and then cuts toward the goalpost

bomb ▶ a very long pass

fade ▶ a route in which the receiver runs toward the back corner of the end zone

slant ▶ a route in which the receiver goes across the field on a diagonal path

A **wideout** like Cooper Kupp can make all kinds of trouble for a defense. The Los Angeles Rams receiver had a huge year in 2021. He led the NFL in passes caught and receiving yards. He also showed he could do it all.

FACT A buttonhook was a common tool back in the 1800s. Most households had one. They were used to fasten the buttons on shoes and other clothing. The tool commonly had a wooden handle with a steel hook on one end. Its shape inspired the name of a passing play in football.

Quarterback Matthew Stafford was new to the Rams that season. He looked for Kupp in all kinds of situations. Facing a tough third down, Stafford often threw to Kupp. The receiver was known for running perfect routes. He could get himself open on a **hitch** or a **buttonhook**. He could also get behind the defensive backs on a **deep post** route. If Stafford threw a **bomb**, Kupp was usually his target.

Kupp proved to be especially strong in the red zone. That's the name for the area between the opposing team's 20-yard line and the goal line. Why is it called the red zone? Think of a flashing red warning light. For the defense, the red zone is dangerous ground. Kupp ran **fades**. He ran **slants**. He ran all sorts of routes. He did anything he could to get the TD.

Los Angeles Rams wide receiver Cooper Kupp makes a catch against the Cincinnati Bengals.

flea-flicker ▶ a play in which the quarterback hands off to a running back, the running back charges ahead, then stops and tosses the ball back to the quarterback

reverse ▶ a play in which the quarterback hands the ball to a runner heading in one direction, and he gives the ball to another runner going the other way; the goal is to confuse the defense about who has the ball

Hail Mary ▶ a long pass thrown toward the end zone at the end of a half or a game

Sometimes coaches must do something unusual to improve their team's luck. If the other team's defense seems to have control, a **flea-flicker** or a **reverse** might change things. Both of them are trick plays. And both are meant to confuse a defense. These trick plays can produce big gains. They can also backfire.

Kyler Murray and DeAndre Hopkins have been part of some thrilling plays in the NFL. Murray plays quarterback for the Arizona Cardinals. Hopkins is his wide receiver. They can make any defense miserable.

In 2020, the pair connected on a legendary play. In a game against the Buffalo Bills, the Cardinals were down by four points with only seconds remaining. The Cardinals had to try a **Hail Mary** pass. A Hail Mary is not a trick play. It's a desperation play.

Hopkins catches the game-winning touchdown pass against the Buffalo Bills in 2020.

The play began near midfield. Murray rolled out to his left as Hopkins sprinted toward the end zone. Murray escaped a tackler and launched a long pass. The ball traveled 50 yards through the air. In the end zone, three defenders surrounded Hopkins. But the receiver outjumped his opponents. He grabbed the ball and fell to the turf with it in his hands.

The Cardinals' prayers were answered. The touchdown gave them the victory. And the play soon became known as the Hail Murray.

FACT Many people say Cowboys quarterback Roger Staubach made the Hail Mary pass famous. In the 1975 playoffs, Staubach threw a long touchdown pass to Drew Pearson in the final seconds to defeat the Minnesota Vikings. After the game, Staubach said, "Well, I guess you could call it a Hail Mary. You throw it up and pray."

CHAPTER TWO
GETTING DEFENSIVE

blitz ▶ a defensive play in which one or more linebackers or defensive backs cross the line of scrimmage to pursue the quarterback; the word comes from the German *Blitzkrieg*, meaning "lightning war"

neutral zone ▶ a thin strip of space running across the field; when the ball is placed before a play, only the center can be in this space

trenches ▶ the area at the line of scrimmage where offensive and defensive linemen collide

sack ▶ tackling the quarterback behind the line of scrimmage

Sometimes people speak about football like it is warfare. Quarterbacks throw bombs. Defenders **blitz** the quarterback. Linemen face off across the **neutral zone**. Games are won and lost in the **trenches**.

It's easy to think of opposing teams like two armies. But football is only a game, of course. It's not war. Still, the language of battle comes naturally when talking about defense.

Myles Garrett and T.J. Watt are among the NFL's best defensive players. Garrett plays defensive end for the Cleveland Browns. Watt plays linebacker for the Pittsburgh Steelers.

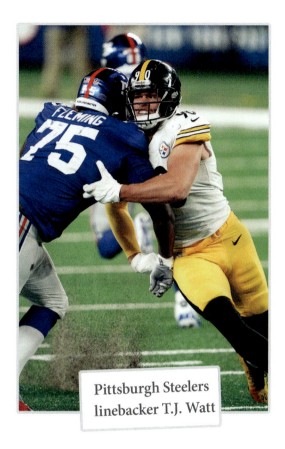

Pittsburgh Steelers linebacker T.J. Watt

Watt's power and strength put him among the league leaders in **sacks** and tackles each season. In 2020, Watt led the league in tackles for a loss. That means he stopped the ballcarrier behind the line of scrimmage. And he did so more than anyone else.

Garrett helped the Browns become a winner after years of struggle. In 2020, he led the Browns to the playoffs. It was the team's first postseason game in 18 years. The following season, Garrett became the team's sack king. He set a new Browns record for sacks in a single season.

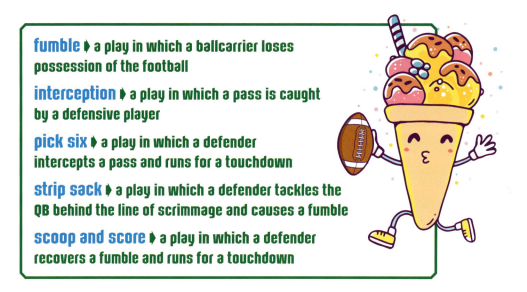

fumble ▶ a play in which a ballcarrier loses possession of the football

interception ▶ a play in which a pass is caught by a defensive player

pick six ▶ a play in which a defender intercepts a pass and runs for a touchdown

strip sack ▶ a play in which a defender tackles the QB behind the line of scrimmage and causes a fumble

scoop and score ▶ a play in which a defender recovers a fumble and runs for a touchdown

For a defense, almost nothing beats the thrill of taking the ball away from the offense. Defenders love to jump on a **fumble** or grab an **interception**. It's even better if that interception becomes a **pick six**. Same goes for a **strip sack** that becomes a **scoop and score**.

At his peak, Cam Newton was among the best quarterbacks in the NFL. But a pair of fumbles in the Super Bowl marred his best year. In 2015, Newton was voted the NFL's most valuable player. He led the Carolina Panthers to a 15–1 record in the regular season. After two playoff wins, the Panthers faced the Denver Broncos in Super Bowl 50.

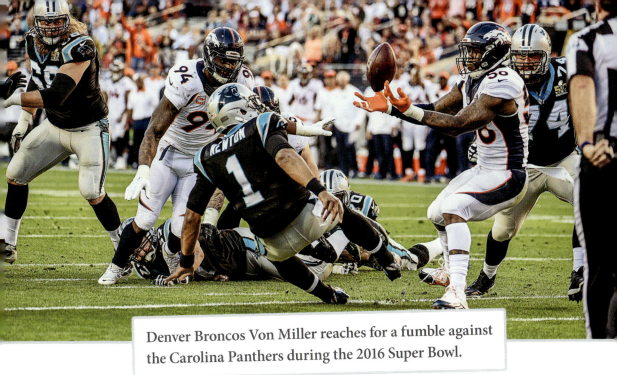

Denver Broncos Von Miller reaches for a fumble against the Carolina Panthers during the 2016 Super Bowl.

That's where Newton ran into Von Miller. A star linebacker for the Broncos, Miller changed the game by forcing Newton to fumble twice. In the first quarter, Miller got a strip sack at the Panthers' 5-yard line. The ball bounced into the end zone. One of Miller's teammates scooped up the ball for a touchdown. Later in the game, Miller again batted the ball out of Newton's hands. The play nearly turned into a scoop and score. Defensive back T.J. Ward grabbed the ball but went down a few yards short of the goal line.

The Broncos won the game 24–10. Newton's legendary season ended on a sour note.

audible ▸ when the quarterback changes the call at the line of scrimmage by calling out a new play

shutdown corner ▸ a cornerback who can defend the other team's best receiver effectively each week

ballhawk ▸ a player skilled at intercepting passes or breaking up pass plays

play-action pass ▸ a play in which the quarterback fakes a handoff to a running back before throwing a pass

hitting pay dirt ▸ reaching the end zone for a touchdown; in the gold rush, hitting pay dirt meant striking it rich

Tom Brady has been making defenses suffer for years. He spent 20 seasons with the New England Patriots. He led the team to the Super Bowl nine times. The Pats won six of those games. In 2020, Brady moved to the Tampa Bay Buccaneers. At age 43, he guided the Bucs to a Super Bowl win.

How does he do it? Brady has serious skills. Obviously. But he has shown shortcomings, especially as he's aged. He doesn't have the speed of Patrick Mahomes. He doesn't dodge pass rushers with the skill of Aaron Rodgers. But Brady makes the most of his experience to beat a defense. He won't hesitate to call an **audible** at the line, and he makes smart choices with the ball.

Dallas Cowboys players celebrate after Trevon Diggs (7) intercepted a pass against the Tampa Bay Buccaneers in 2021.

To stop Brady, the defense has to do something special. A fierce pass rush helps. And a **shutdown corner** can make a big difference. Trevon Diggs burst onto the NFL scene in 2021. The Dallas Cowboys cornerback is a total **ballhawk**. He's not easily fooled by a **play-action pass**. And he follows receivers like a shadow. Diggs led the league in interceptions in 2021. And he frustrated lots of quarterbacks.

When Brady and Diggs met early that season, Diggs had one interception and broke up two other passes. But Brady got the last laugh. His team **hit pay dirt** on four of his passes, and the Bucs won 31–29.

Will ▸ weak-side linebacker

Mike ▸ middle linebacker

Sam ▸ strong-side linebacker

high-motor guy ▸ a hardworking player who never quits

Will, Mike, and Sam are all linebackers in the NFL. Bobby Wagner is a Mike. Fred Warner is also a Mike. In the language of the game, a Mike is a middle linebacker. A Sam is a strong-side linebacker. A Will is a weak-side linebacker.

Most NFL teams play with four defensive linemen and three linebackers. The strong-side linebacker goes on the side of the field where the offense has the most players. Usually that means he lines up across from the tight end. The weak-side linebacker goes on the other side of the formation. Of course, the middle linebacker plays between the others.

FACT The strong-side linebacker often gets the glory. He's the one most likely to rush the quarterback. He has to make a lot of tackles. The weak-side linebacker might be a bit smaller and faster. Often he has to fall back and cover pass receivers.

Warner and Wagner stand out among all linebackers in the NFL. Wagner has been the anchor of the Seattle Seahawks' defense for years. He joined the team in 2012. He quickly became a star. He made the Pro Bowl eight times in his first nine seasons. Warner hasn't been in the league as long. He arrived as a rookie with the San Francisco 49ers in 2018. Before his fourth season began, he became the highest-paid linebacker in pro football.

Warner and Wagner lead their defenses on the field. They call the defensive plays. And they have to do it all. They rush the quarterback. They tackle runners. They cover receivers. Both of them are **high-motor guys**. They never take a play off.

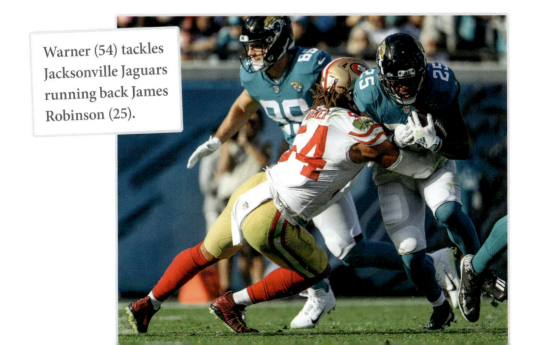

Warner (54) tackles Jacksonville Jaguars running back James Robinson (25).

CHAPTER THREE
BOOT IT!

gridiron ▸ a football field; the nickname arose because the striped field looks something like a grate used for cooking over a fire

pooch ▸ a short, high punt or kickoff; the goal of a pooch kick is to force someone other than a speedy kick returner to field the ball for the opposing team

squib kick ▸ a low kick that usually bounces along the turf; as with a pooch, the goal of a squib kick is to force someone other than a speedy returner to field the ball

shank ▸ a kick that goes in an unintended direction

Punters and placekickers are the oddballs of the **gridiron**. They are usually the smallest guys on the team. Sometimes they do curious things, such as **pooch** punts and **squib kicks**. Also, kickers and punters spend little time on the field. NFL punters average less than four punts per game. Placekickers try an average of about two field goals per game.

Still, kickers and punters are the subject of lots of talk. They find ways to drive coaches mad. A punter might **shank** one and give the other team great field position. A placekicker might miss a short field goal with the game on the line.

In 2016, for example, Blair Walsh of the Minnesota Vikings goofed at the worst possible time. He missed a 27-yard try for a field goal with 26 seconds left in a playoff game. The Vikings lost by a single point.

Kickers can be heroes too. In 2021, the Ravens trailed the Detroit Lions by a single point. Only three seconds remained in the game. Justin Tucker jogged onto the field to try a 66-yard field goal. He booted it with all his might. The ball hit the crossbar. Then it bounced through the goalposts. The Ravens had won the game. And Tucker had set a new record for the longest field goal in NFL history.

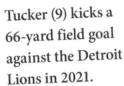

Tucker (9) kicks a 66-yard field goal against the Detroit Lions in 2021.

FACT In 1969, Steve O'Neal of the New York Jets made the longest punt in NFL history. From his own end zone, the rookie launched a 98-yard punt. The ball went about 68 yards through the air and rolled another 30 yards.

extra point ▸ a point after touchdown, or PAT; immediately following a touchdown, the offense can try a short kick for one point

gunner ▸ a player on kickoffs and punts whose job is to sprint down the field and go directly for the kick returner

juke ▸ a move made by a football player who wants to fake out an opposing player and run past him

ankle tackle ▸ a play in which a defender grabs a runner at his ankles or sweeps at his feet to bring him down

Players on special teams are on the field for kickoffs and punts. They also handle field-goal and **extra-point** tries. Kickers and punters have key roles, of course. **Gunners**, kick returners, and punt returners also have important jobs. Really, though, a mistake by anyone on special teams can be costly.

Consider the example of a 95-yard punt return by Tyreek Hill in 2017. Hill is a star wide receiver for the Kansas City Chiefs. He's known for his blazing speed. He can also **juke** his way around would-be tacklers. Early in his pro career, the Chiefs also used him as a punt returner. And he was a good one.

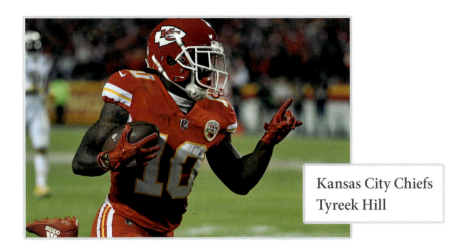

Kansas City Chiefs
Tyreek Hill

Hill was a rookie that season in 2017. The Chiefs were facing the San Diego Chargers in a big game to finish the regular season. Hill dropped back near his goal line to receive a third-quarter punt. He caught the ball at the 5-yard line. He faked to his left, then dashed to his right. He broke free of an **ankle tackle** and took off along the sideline. Near midfield he had to push his own teammate out of the way.

Then he was gone for the TD. And the Chiefs were headed to the playoffs.

FACT Devin Hester might have been the greatest punt returner in NFL history. Hester played 11 seasons in the league, including eight with the Chicago Bears. He scored 14 touchdowns on punt returns. That's a record that has stood since 2014. He also scored five times on kickoff returns.

CHAPTER FOUR

ZEBRAS AND ACES

holding ▶ when a player grabs an opponent who doesn't have the ball; called on offensive or defensive players

horse-collar tackle ▶ when a defender grabs an offensive player's back collar or shoulder pads at the back of his neck and pulls him down

false start ▶ a movement made by any offensive player other than the center after the ball has been placed and the offense has taken position to start a play; the play begins when the center snaps the ball

In the NFL, a **horse-collar tackle** will cause a zebra to throw a flag. Football officials wear shirts with black and white stripes. That's why they are sometimes called zebras. It's a childish nickname, but it stuck.

Seven officials are on the field for an NFL game. That number includes one referee. The referee is in charge of the crew of officials. They announce each penalty that is called. They also stand out because they wear a white cap. All other officials wear black caps.

Down judge Sarah Thomas during a game between the Dallas Cowboys and New York Giants in 2021

The remaining officials include the umpire, line judge, down judge, field judge, side judge, and back judge. The referee and umpire stand behind the offense at the beginning of each play. The back judge stands behind the defense. The others are positioned along the sidelines.

Any of the officials can call a penalty. If an official sees a player break a rule, they toss a small yellow flag onto the field. **Holding** and **false start** are among the most common penalties. Horse-collar tackles are rare.

The language of football is always changing. Long ago, a star football player might have been called a grid ace. Wide receivers were called flankers. A running back or other ballcarrier might have been called a leather lugger.

In the early NFL, no one ever mentioned a receiver's YAC. That's a newer bit of football talk. It stands for "yards after catch." Wide receivers and other pass catchers are now judged by YAC. The statistic shows the yardage they gain from the spot where they caught a pass. Players skilled at breaking tackles or dodging tacklers rack up big YAC totals.

No one talked about YAC when Don Hutson was piling up receiving yards in the 1930s. The Green Bay Packers star was perhaps the NFL's first great receiver. He held 18 league records when he retired from the game. He knew how to handle the pigskin.

Don Hutson, 1930s

That is among the many things that have not changed. Fans have called the ball a pigskin as long as anyone can remember. The game of football has thrilled them for just as long.

Glossary

airborne (AYR-born)—being in the air or off the ground

backfield (BAK-feeld)—the football players who line up behind the line of scrimmage

backfire (BAK-fyre)—to have a result opposite to what was planned

crossbar (KROSS-bahr)—the horizontal bar at the bottom of the upright goalposts on both ends of the football field

desperation (dess-puhr-RAY-shuhn)—a loss of hope and surrender to misery or dread

formation (fohr-MAY-shuhn)—the arrangement or grouping of persons on the football field

opponent (uh-POH-nuhnt)—a person or thing that opposes another

outlaw (OWT-lah)—a lawless person or one who is running away from the law

Read More

Editors of Sports Illustrated Kids. *The Greatest Football Teams of All Time.* New York: Liberty Street, an imprint of Time Inc. Books, 2018.

Pryor, Shawn. *Football's Sickest Sacks!* North Mankato, MN: Capstone Press, 2021.

Storden, Thom. *Big-Time Football Records.* North Mankato, MN: Capstone Press, 2022.

Internet Sites

National Football League
nfl.com

Pro Football Hall of Fame
profootballhof.com

Sports Illustrated Kids: Football
sikids.com/football

Index

About the Author

Martin Driscoll is a former newspaper reporter and longtime editor of children's books. He is also the author of several sports books for children, including biographies of legendary stars of boxing, baseball, and basketball. Driscoll lives in Southern Minnesota with his wife and two children.